DEE SELLERS

OUCH!
Copyright © 2020 by Dee Sellers
Email: made2survive@gmail.com

Edited by Melane Bower
Cover and page layout by majonesdesigns.com

All Rights Reserved
Unless otherwise indicated, all Scripture quotations are taken from the *New King James Version* of the Bible.
Contents and/or cover may not be reproduced in whole or in part in any form without the express written consent of the Publisher.

ISBN 978-1-7322783-0-1

*Printed in the United States of America.*

# CONTENT

ACKNOWLEDGEMENTS ................................................. 6
PREFACE ............................................................................ 8
CHAPTER ONE ................................................................ 10
CHAPTER TWO ............................................................... 15
CHAPTER THREE ............................................................ 18
CHAPTER FOUR .............................................................. 29
CHAPTER FIVE ................................................................ 31
CHAPTER SIX ................................................................... 34
CHAPTER SEVEN ............................................................ 40
CHAPTER EIGHT ............................................................. 45
CHAPTER NINE ............................................................... 50
CHAPTER TEN ................................................................. 53
CHAPTER ELEVEN .......................................................... 55
CHAPTER TWELVE ......................................................... 58
CHAPTER THIRTEEN ..................................................... 61
CHAPTER FOURTEEN .................................................... 64
CHAPTER FIFTEEN ......................................................... 68
EPILOGUE ........................................................................ 71

# ACKNOWLEDGEMENTS

First of all, I honor God for dropping this book into my spirit more than thirty years ago. "Ouch" is dedicated to the memory of my late parents, Elder Ureese and Martha Chillis. To my sisters, Mary Davenport and Cathleen Chillis (now deceased). To my heartbeat and only biological daughter, Kesha M. Thomas, and my grandson, Michael Thomas II. To my godchildren, that have always respected me as God-mommy; Disa Stephenson, Kendal Green, Terrell Smith, Jonathan Edwards, Tierra and Tiana Brinson, Ires Singleton, Jada Parham. My friend and brother, Pastor Michael Coe, Apostle Patricia A. Phillips, Bishop Pamela D. Herndon, Pastor Barbara Adams, Rochelle Singleton, and Pastor Lois Alexander, who would from time to time encourage me to write the book. To my sisters/cousins, Dr. Rose Perry, Mrs. Toni Davis, Mrs. Evetta Hall, Tina Moon, and to Lady Janice Parham.

Thanks to all of you, that did and continue to hold me up in prayer and words of encouragement.

# PREFACE

*"I will bless the Lord at all times; and his praise shall continually be in my mouth."* Psalms 34:1

The Lord dropped the title of this book in my spirit more than thirty years ago. "OUCH!" At that time, I was clueless about what was in store for my life. Having given my life to Christ at the age of fourteen, raised in a sanctified household, knew how to do church, jump shout, sing on the choir, ya da, ya da, ya da, I knew enough to realize that being "saved" would not be a bed of roses on a regular basis. I had no idea of the hurt, disappointments, struggles, and sickness that I would have to face. By no means is this book written to bash or defame any person. It is simple my story; nothing fictitious, just my story.

My desire in writing "OUCH" is to encourage men and women, despite what you face in life, that: *"Being confident of this, that he who began a good work in you will carry it on to completion until the day of Christ Jesus."* (Philippians 1:6)

# CHAPTER ONE

I was born and raised in Buffalo, New York. My father, the late Elder Uresse Chillis, was the founder and pastor of the New Hope COGIC My mother, of course, was the First Lady, but back in the 1960's, many, if not most, First Ladies were not acknowledged as they are today.

New Hope was pretty much a family church. If you weren't related by blood, you soon became part of the family regardless. Along with my sisters, Mary and Cathleen (Cat), I was raised in a very strict home setting. Our lives primarily consisted of school and church. You did not spend the night away from home; you ate and played at home. I recall when I would ask Mom if I could go over to one of my "church" friend's house; her response was: "You ain't lose nothing at Sister_____'s house and don't ask me that again or else I'm going to whip your butt." We could go over to other family members' houses but when the streetlight came on, "You better be in this house!"

My outlet was attending Elementary Public School #37. I was one of if not the biggest troublemaker that attended 37. There were days, even weeks, when I spent more time in the principal's office than I did in the classroom. I never liked bullies, so for many of my friends I felt it was my responsibility to protect them, not only from other kids, but even the teachers. One day

# OUCH

in fifth grade, my teacher slammed the pointer stick on the desk of one of the shyest girls in the school, telling her that the next time the stick came down it would connect with her hand. I knew quite well that I was going to get in trouble and be sent to Principal's office, my father would be called to come pick me up from school, and when Mom came home I would get a whipping, but at that moment none of that mattered. I jumped out of my desk (not my business), grabbed the pointer from the teacher, broke it in half, threw it at him, and suggested that if he wanted to hit somebody, "Hit me."

I wanted a life outside of church, so I tried to get connected with gangs like the Junior Black Panthers, knowing without a doubt I would have to keep a low profile. (Did I mention that my mama didn't play?) Living in the Fruit Belt section of Buffalo, many of the Junior Black Panthers attended School #37, which made it easy for me to act out while in school. Thinking back, I simply wanted a way out of the "church life"; I wanted to belong to something or someone that had nothing to do with "church."

Being a P.K. (Preacher's Kid), there was a certain standard that I believed was expected of my sisters and me. Back in the 1960's, you weren't asked to do certain things, you were told. And unlike the twenty first century church, you did not ask "Why?" "How come?" "When? or "Where?", you did what you were told and did it to the best of your ability. I honestly believe that before I learned my ABC's, I had already memorized Psalms 23.

Back then, the second Sunday in June was known as "Children's Day," the day where kids were in charge of the entire service from Sunday school to the end of Sunday evening, so at the age of six I preached my first sermon: "The Lord is my

Shepherd, I shall not want." With that being said, I realized that the hand of God was on my life at an early age, but the reality is that I wanted to do me and what I considered as having fun.

My father, the late Elder Ureese Chillis, was known throughout the Church of God in Christ as a man of prayer. His legacy lives on today in the city of Buffalo and in the lives of many of us that grew up, moved to different states, and became members of thriving non-denominational churches as well as those that are still COGIC. The theme of New Hope became "HAVE YOU PRAYED ABOUT IT?" On Monday through Saturday, if you were not working, you would be in morning prayer. For those of us that were in school, every Saturday we had to be on our knees in prayer from 9AM until 10AM. During the summer months when schools were closed, we were in prayer from 9AM to 10AM, Monday through Saturday. No sleeping was allowed, as my father would walk the floor making sure we were awake and praying. Today I can honestly say I thank God for those early morning prayers, because they taught me how to not merely say prayers but to pray until I touched the heart of God. I would even venture to say that those that grew up under Chillis' ministry learned the power of prayer and how to get a prayer through. We were taught to pray with power and authority, as well as to pray the Word of God, back to God.

As I entered my teenage years, I was excited because, in my mind, I was getting closer to becoming an adult, which meant I could do what I wanted, when I wanted. But I was still living in my parent's house and their rules remained the same, which meant you were going to be saved, live holy, and go to church. Now just to set the record straight, I never considered my mother or father as being abusive or mean. My parents took good

# OUCH

care of us, they just raised us how they thought was right: to love God, His Word, and His people. We never went without a meal but when it came to disrespect or talking back, it was not allowed. One of the many conversations I recall having with Mama was the day I turned thirteen and my period started. There was no previous conversation of what to expect, so when it happened, I was somewhat afraid and didn't know what to do. I went to Mary and told her what was going on, and she gave me the supplies I needed and told me I had to tell Mom. The conversation with Mom was very short and to the point: "Keep your dress down and your panties up and don't let them little mannish boys be kissing on you. If you end up pregnant, I'm going to put you in Booth." (Booth was a home for teenage unwed mothers.) I was determined not to get pregnant and be put out of my house. One day in school, a guy surprisingly kissed me on the cheek. I tried to beat the brakes off him. I thought that kiss on the cheek got me pregnant!

Going into high school (and there were several that I could have attended), I wanted to go to East High, as my understanding at the time was that was where the "wild" kids went. However, Martha was not having it. My sister Mary was in her last year at Fosdick Masten Vocational High School, and as far as Mom was concerned that was where I was going too. I recall Mom saying to me, "You just want to go to the East to be around them bad boys and 'fast-tail' little girls. I'm not having it!" Fosdick Masten, also known as Girls High, was without question an ALL GIRLS School which offered several technical vocational studies.

Thinking back, attending Girls High really wasn't bad at all. I continued to do the same thing I had done in elementary school; the difference was, I only had to fight all girls instead of boys and girls. Ms. Bruckheimer, who happened to have been Mary's typing teacher, had no problem telling me what a good student Mary was in comparison to me. And me being me at that time, I felt I needed to reintroduce myself to her by letting her know, "That's why they call me Dee-Dee and my sister's name is Mary." (If my mom had known how disrespectful I was to my teachers, I promise you, I would have been made to stand up for weeks at a time!)

Now again, to set the record straight, I never considered my mother as being abusive or mean. I believe my parents saw something in me as to how God would use me in and for the Kingdom, something that at the time I could not imagine. God use me in ministry for His glory? The Apostle Paul says this: *"In him, we were also chosen, having been predestined according to the plan of him who works out everything in conformity with the purpose of his will, in order that we who were in the first to hope in Christ, might be for the praise of his glory."* (Ephesians 1:11-12-- NIV). Even now, there are times when I pause and meditate on the very fact that God would choose me, before I was born.

# CHAPTER TWO

At the age of fourteen, I found myself in church on a Saturday night. Of course, that was nothing new because whenever there was a church service, we were there–no questions asked, no answers given, we HAD to be present and on time. This particular service was life changing, for myself as well as approximately thirty other young people. It was a musical service, and as the group was singing, a young lady (who looked older than she actually was) walked into the church and proceeded up the center aisle. She was drunk, and the strong smell of liquor that reeked from her body was amazing. She fell to her knees and cried out, "God, please help me!" Needless to say, the musical portion of the service ended and the "tarry service" began. Thirty of us knew how to clap in time, knew how to dance and shout, and some could even bring forth the Word, but we did not know Jesus as our Lord and Savior.

Tarry service, what does that mean? I'm glad you asked. During that time, we were taught and believed that in order to be saved you had to get on your knees and repeatedly ask Jesus to save your soul. Everyone on the altar would all be saying the same thing while the older saints would pray with us, saying, "Save me Jesus, save me Jesus!" This could go on for one or two hours. If you really got into it, you would roll around on the floor, hence the term "holy rollers." When we got up, we were asked the question, "How do you feel?" If the answer was anything other than, "I believe the Lord saved me tonight," we were told to come back the next night and do it all over again. Once you said you were saved you then had to "tarry" for the baptism of the Holy Ghost. Once I spoke in "unknown tongues," I was told I had the Holy Ghost.

Please understand that those old saints, which I honor and respect to this day, taught us based on their learning and understanding and how they were taught. They were very stringent in their teaching and what they believed. They taught us that ladies did not wear pants because it was an abomination to God. We weren't allowed to wear lipstick and wearing anything red in color was out of the question; if you did, you were going to die and go to hell. That applied to both men and women. Scriptures were unintentionally taken out of context, which prevented us from going to the movies, ball games, or any outside activity that was considered sinful. One scripture frequently used was, *"Blessed is the man who does not walk in the counsel of the wicked or stands in the way of sinners or sit in the seat of mockers."* (Psalms 1:1)

That night in June was life changing for me, because despite the "tarrying" and yes, even the rolling around on the floor, I accepted Jesus Christ into my life as my Lord and Savior. It was then that my desire and longing for more of God, His will, and His Word increased. I had seen God perform miracles in our services before, like when one of the missionaries was scheduled for surgery. During one of our weeknight services, the praise was high (my playing church became real), and the missionary was rejoicing when suddenly she ran out to the bathroom. When she came back in, she said the tumors dropped in the toilet!

# OUCH

Needless to say, we almost tore that little storefront church up. Some of the other miracles included the time when one of the young guys developed alopecia and Pastor Chillis prayed and laid hands all over his head. When we came back to the next service, he walked in with the biggest grin and a head full of hair. The last one I will mention was when one of my little cousins, Tina, was born with feet deformities and the doctors declared that she would never walk. Once again, during a mighty outpouring of God's presence and the saints praising God, my father called for Tina to be brought to him. He anointed her legs and feet with anointing oil. The next time Tina came to church, they put her down at the entrance to the sanctuary, and as that baby walked up the center aisle of the New Hope COGIC, the church exploded in praise. Even today, Tina still walks and loves the Lord.

I would be so amazed at how I would see God work through and use my father, not to mention his prayer life, that I asked God to use me like He used my dad.

A word of caution: Be careful what you ask God for...he just might give you what you asked of Him.

# CHAPTER THREE

Elder Chillis wanted the young people to learn and experience as much as we could about the Church of God in Christ. We started traveling to the Youth Congress, a national and international gathering of young people who traveled once a year to a different state and city. It was amazing to see saved young people gather from all over the world.

When I was sixteen, the Youth Congress was held in Milwaukee, Wisconsin. It was there that my eyes connected with a young man from Philadelphia, Pennsylvania. We began to stay in touch through letters and frequent phone calls, and eventually become boyfriend and girlfriend. He would make visits to Buffalo to see me. George (not his real name) was a preacher and loved to praise God. We would pray together on the phone and constantly talk about the Word. I would go on my personal consecrations because I knew if I were to get married, I wanted it to be for life. The more intense my heart got into this relationship the more earnestly I would pray, asking God that if he wasn't the one, to let either me or my father know.

I graduated high school in 1970, went on to practical nursing school, and graduated from there in 1971. I worked hard at Veterans Memorial Hospital as well as a nursing home, because by now I had been proposed to and George and I were getting mar-

# OUCH

ried. I was a virgin and was leaving not only my natural family but my church family as well. I had been raised as a stay at home girl, and moving to Philadelphia, Pennsylvania was not just a life changing move, it was a gigantic move that I was not prepared for on many levels. I became Mrs. Sellers, the wife of a preacher, and I was convinced that I was married "till death do us part."

One of the first surprises I experienced after moving to Philly was living in an apartment where the bathroom was down the hall. George had told my parents and me that he was moving us into a two-bedroom apartment that was fully furnished. Upon my arrival to my "new home," I literally had to walk past the bedroom before reaching the inside of the apartment. When George opened the door to the living room, there was no living room—I was smack dab in the bedroom. There was no living room and no living room furniture. The kitchen was equipped with a round piece of plywood that sat on blocks. To my knowledge this was the first lie that I realized George had told me, but I was determined that divorce was not a part of my destiny and I was going to work through this and save my marriage.

George worked in Trenton, New Jersey from 3 pm to 11 pm. We didn't have a car (he didn't have a license at the time) so he would commute back and forth every day, usually leaving home around 1pm and returning home 2am or 3am the following morning. My days were very long and lonesome. There was one lady, Dill, from my new church, PFT, that sort of took me under her wings, invited me to her family functions, ya da, ya da, ya da. To this day she remains one of my closest and dearest friends.

Within several months of moving to Philly, I realized that I needed to get a job and I needed one sooner than later. I refused to continue walking down a hallway to take care of my personal hygiene and bathing needs, not knowing when I would run into other tenants in the building. I got a job at Methodist Hospital as a nursing assistant, where I met some great people and enjoyed going to work. It was better than staying in that apartment day after day. I learned my way around Philadelphia quickly, including riding the trolley cars, the Broad Street subway, and sometimes the Frankford trains.

Around the sixth month of marriage, George's job was having a Christmas party, which he wanted me to attend. I was somewhat elated, because other than going to church when he had to preach and he wanted me to sing, we hardly ever went anywhere together. (I guess you could say I was beyond naïve.) However, George asked me to do something weird which I refused to do. He bought me a maternity dress and wanted me to tie a pillow around my stomach to give the appearance that I was pregnant. First clue, when I got to Trenton, he was furious with me. "Why didn't you wear the dress I bought you, and why don't you look like you are pregnant?"

"Because I'm not and you and I both know that," I answered. "Why do you want me to pretend something that is not true?" He refused to answer, and as a matter of fact he requested that I leave and not attend the party. I was heartbroken, to say the least. My stubbornness would not let him do this, not this time, not to mention I had traveled via trains all the way from West Philly to Trenton, New Jersey. He was furious, and I had a ball at the party. (Every month, I was asked the question, "Are you pregnant yet?" and every month my excuse (with somewhat of a sad face) was, "No baby, we didn't get it right this month.")

Shortly after that escapade I found out that I really was

# OUCH

pregnant, but I miscarried in the first trimester, which George blamed me for. Having a miscarriage was a hard pill to swallow by itself but being told that I caused it made me feel worthless. I wondered to myself, "What can I do to make him happy again? What can I do to make him love me again?" He wanted me to get pregnant immediately after the miscarriage. But, did I mention that my mama was a wise woman and taught me well? I knew my body on the inside needed time to heal. I also knew it would take time emotionally and with George being so moody, I didn't know if I wanted to have a baby because I didn't want to have to raise a child by myself.

In 1974, I went to the National Convocation of the Church of God in Christ and met up with my family from Buffalo. One day at the Morrison cafeteria while having dinner with family, my father looked across the table at me. "Does your mama know you're pregnant?" His words shocked me so much that I jumped up from the table, ran to the bathroom, and brought up everything I had just eaten. I didn't realize I was pregnant and for the life of me could not understand why he said that. Of course, I denied being pregnant and inquired why he would say that. Dad said, "I see the baby's heartbeat in your neck." Somewhat in a state of shock and disbelief, I decided I would leave Memphis earlier than planned. I wanted to go home and tell George what my dad had told me and make an appointment with my gynecologist to see if it was true.

What a devastation I experienced when I opened the door to the apartment! George was asleep in bed, wrapped up in the arms of a man! I backed out of the door and locked it, then put my hand over my mouth as tears ran down my face. Deep depression set in. I began to wonder what was wrong with me, was this my fault? I even asked God to forgive me. Certainly, it had to be my fault that George would turn to a man. After all, he was a man of God, he was saved, I was saved. My mind was on a winding roller coaster and George was controlling the ride.

By this time, although mentally there were days when I felt as if I was going to lose my mind, spiritually I was experiencing growing pains. My spiritual gift of exhortation had not been revealed to myself or anyone else. I would be asked to be mistress of ceremony for the renowned Savettes Choir as well as at other anniversary and banquet affairs. Having preached my first message around six years old, I had no idea that preaching the gospel would become my forte. The more I was asked to preside over a service, the more resentful my husband became. If he came to a service in which I would preside, the Spirit of God would use me. I would give a word of encouragement and the church would respond with shouting and dancing, glorifying God. I didn't then, and still don't to this day, ever take credit for or take for granted how God uses me. I was just grateful that He chose me.

When we got home, there was hell—and I do mean hell—to pay for it. Such ugly words would spew out of George's mouth, words that were meant to crush me as a woman. God would continue to use me, yet my determination to hold my marriage together persisted. After all, I had prayed and fasted about this before I got married, and I was convinced that he was for me and I was for him. The jealously that he felt became more and more heart wrenching. Although I believed he was a good preacher in his own right, he would tell me that people he had introduced me to enjoyed me more than him. Although I never have and never will look at preaching the gospel of Jesus Christ as a competitive sport, evidently George did. He would not support me in anything concerning the church. Occasionally he would still ask me to accompany him to one of his preaching engagements, to sing before he would preach. But if people enjoyed my solo that became a problem as well, and he not only stopped asking me to go with him completely but would not even tell me when he had an engagement.

I continued working at Methodist Hospital, where each day I came home and cooked. For the first six months of marriage we were happy, or so I thought, although George continued to take his weekend trips. By April of 1975, I was enormous in size, as the baby was really growing to the point that I had to stop working. On my last day at Methodist, I had to get a cab home because of the many, many gifts I had received from my co-workers. With excitement, I figured George and I would sit and look through the gifts together. I thought it would be fun and something we both would take pleasure in doing, but not so. He came home, no kiss on the cheek, no "How was your last day at work?", no "What's for dinner? or "Are we going out?" There was nothing. Have you ever sat in a place of "nothing"? As I tried to analyze what was happening, I fixed his plate of food and right before my eyes, he dumped the entire meal in the trash. Convincing myself that he must be coming down with a stomach virus, I tried not to display my disappointment.

By that time, he had quit his job in Trenton and was working at Jefferson University Hospital in Philadelphia. When he came home from work, I was there each day to greet him with open arms, because in June we would welcome our baby into this world, our world. However, he would walk pass me as if I did not exist. I would speak, he would not reply; I would cook, he would either throw the meal in the trash or just leave it on the table. He would stay on the phone for hours but not communicate with me at all. So, I got smart and thanks to Ma Bell, I learned how to disconnect the phone line by the time he got home so that he was unable to talk on the phone. He would get heated, but I figured that two could play this game as well as one. When he would leave for work the following morning, I would reconnect the wire so that I could talk to my family and friends.

If I asked him a question, it was as if I had not said anything. He seemed to despise me, and I couldn't for the life of me figure out why. From the latter half of April, the entire month of May, and until June ninth, it was as if I did not exist. (By the way, June ninth would have been our anniversary.) One day when George came home from work, I was determined to find out what was going on with him; I was not going to deal with his silent treatment anymore. He raised his hand to hit me. My instincts kicked in right away. As his hand was coming down, I grabbed his arm with the suggestion that, "If you're going to hit me, please kill me because if you hit me and I live, I'm going to jail." He walked out the door. Good choice!

Most of my days were spent in bed or on the sofa that I had worked to buy and to move into an apartment where the bathroom was not down the hallway (hint!). On June 9, 1975, I cringed as I heard George coming up the stairs. The phone was reconnected, and I was sitting in bed watching TV. He walked into the bedroom with the biggest smile on his face. "Hey Babe, I hope you didn't cook today. Let's go out to dinner to celebrate our second anniversary!" In total shock, I leaned over the side of the bed (being careful not to fall) trying to look under the bed to see who he was talking to.

# OUCH

He came up with some lame excuse that the thought of him being a father had overwhelmed him and he was scared. As he asked for forgiveness at the time, not one scripture on forgiveness mattered to me. I brought to his attention how I felt, that I had never given birth to a baby although I knew how to change diapers and to make baby formula from scratch. This thing called motherhood was just as new to me as it was to him. He cried and cried, asking me to forgive him. Remember, there was still this idea in my mind that my marriage was going to last.

We eventually went to dinner, although he did not tell me he had to preach that night and the church had asked him to bring me so that I could sing before he preached. Once again, I sang, the people responded, and he preached a great sermon. Dinner was good, and we went to the movies afterwards and went back home. I was happy again, and looked forward to the birth of my baby and spending the rest of my life as a family with George and Kesha.

On June 21, my labor started, and it was severe. Did I mention that I don't do pain well at all? By the time I got up on Sunday morning, my water had broken and pain hit me like I had never felt before. I made it down to Methodist Hospital, expecting George to be there to hold my hand and rub my back and feet throughout the process of bearing those labor pains—but again, not so. He had to go preach, and I was left by myself.

The labor pains were so intense that even before Kesha came out, I said, "I am one and done!" At one point the pain was so unbearable (so I thought) that I just knew I was going to die in the process. George made it back to the hospital about an hour before I gave birth. By that time, I had been given an epidural to numb me. I was so angry with him that I asked him to leave. "Why are you here now? When I needed you, you weren't here!"

At approximately 8pm, they wheeled me into the delivery suite. George was allowed in at 8:51pm. On June 22, 1975, God gave me the best gift outside of Jesus Christ: a bouncing, screaming baby girl, Kesha Marie Sellers (only I get to call her "Stank"). They quickly took Kesha away and for the next six hours the doctors worked on me, trying to save my life.

My hospital stay turned into five days. The day I came home, my mother flew into Philadelphia from Buffalo to take care of me and her first granddaughter. While Mom was in town, everything was perfect–perfect husband, perfect father, perfect son-in-law. We prayed every night and discussed the Word, but I was somewhat on my "p's and q's." Too much had happened, and I didn't want to be blindsided again.

When Mom left things slowly began to change, and Mr. Perfect left soon after that. Once again there were the silent treatments, once again not eating after I had cooked or even baked a pie or cake from scratch (determination is a powerful thing). Not only did George not want to spend time with me, but he would rarely attend to Kesha. There were times when, if I put her in his lap, he would immediately get up and put her in the crib. He hardly ever came straight home from work; his excuse was that he had to go see his mother. Then there were days when he didn't come home at all. One payday he came home, looking all discombobulated, and told me he'd gotten jumped and the assailants took his entire paycheck. When I suggested that we call the police to report the incident, he strongly suggested that we not. He said they had taken his identification and he was afraid they would come after me. For perhaps a minute I went along with that, until I remembered that he didn't have a driver's license or state ID. All he had was his work badge, and

# OUCH

even I was smart enough to realize they don't put addresses on work identification. Ding, ding, the bell started ringing.

George seemed to be irritated by the very sight of me. Suddenly, he was away from home every other weekend. His excuse was that his pastor was sending him to fill in for her at events. I found that odd, because his pastor was well known as a "preaching machine." Why would she ask him to go and preach for her? After enough of these weekend trips, I noticed that he would receive cards in the mail. One day, he made the mistake of leaving a card on the table. Yes, I read it. I could hardly catch my breath; as a matter of fact, I think I began to hyperventilate. My mind started turning as if I was running a marathon. I read the card over and over and over. It wasn't the reading of the card that caught my attention as much as the written words at the closure: "I love you more than life; we must do this again. Hurry back to me, baby." I was overcome with emotion. I didn't want to believe or accept what was now right before my eyes.

There comes a time in life when, no matter how saved you are or how anointed you may be, you must deal with reality. You can't jump and shout over it, you can't speak in an unknown tongue about it, sometimes you simply must deal with the facts of the matter. The last straw from the broom was when again he went out of town to stand in for his pastor. By that time, I was as hot as fish grease. George called to say that he wasn't coming home until Monday after work.

On Monday morning, I got up early and called George's pastor to ask if I could have a moment of her time. I expressed that as a wife with an infant, I thought it was so unfair of her to always ask my husband to go out of town to preach for her. As I prepared to tell her about the weekend trip he had just made, she stopped me in the middle of what I was saying. She asked if I had heard from George. I told her no, that he said he wouldn't be home until after work. She asked if I had bus fare to meet her at the church, and she would call him and tell him she needed to see him as soon as possible. Of course, I knew he would do that because he really did love his pastor, as did I.

I made babysitting arrangements for Kesha and on the bus I went. I arrived about an hour before George would get there, so that at the pastor's suggestion she and I could have a heart to heart talk. I informed her of the many times George had said he had to go here and there as a favor to her. She in turn told me that she had never sent him to preach in her place, and since he was married with an infant child, she would definitely take that into consideration before asking him to do anything of the sort.

Her office was set up so that when you opened the door you would be facing her, but the sofa on which I was sitting was behind door. George knocked on the door and Pastor invited him in. She began the conversation by asking him how he was doing and that she frequently missed him at church. Caught off guard, he stood there and said, "Well, this weekend I decided to take Dee and the baby away, so we went to Pittsburgh." The pastor looked around at me and said, "I thought you said he left you and the baby at home again?" "That is exactly right," I replied.

Pastor went totally off on George, rebuking him for how he was treating me, for his lack of concern for his family, and for lying and using her name to cause friction in our home. He left the office, and Pastor gave me cab fare. I went to pick up my baby and went home.

By the time George arrived home, he was fuming.

# CHAPTER FOUR

Needless to say, the only noise that was made in the apartment was the baby crying or playing. I had already gone through the silent treatment, so I knew what to look forward to. But not only did he take his negative treatment out on me, he would complain and holler if Kesha cried too long. I never wanted my child to grow up in a family filled with drama. I wasn't raised that way, and neither would my child have to endure such nonsense.

One day, George picked Kesha up out of her crib when she was fretful. He seemed not to be able to calm her down, so he dropped her back in the crib. Yes, I was saved, even preaching a little bit, but you mess with mine you mess with me. The Dee-Dee that I was at Public School #37 rose up and I handled the situation before it got out of control. He never, in a state of being angry, touched my daughter again.

Finally, after about a month he came home and told me, "Get out, go back to Buffalo. I don't want you here or around me anymore. I can't stand to look at you." Devastation took on a new meaning. I was crushed. My heart sank as reality sat in. I didn't know what to do or where to go. Eventually I called one of the church members that lived about two blocks away and told her what was going on. She told me to come to her house, that we could stay there for a while until I figured things out. Although she had a huge house with plenty of room, I was told that my baby (just under one year old) and I could stay in the basement. I was grateful at first, but when I realized that I was staying in an unfinished basement with a water heater and all kinds of pipes, after two nights I had had enough. I expressed my gratitude, gathered the few things that I had taken with me, and returned to the apartment that I had leased in my name only.

When George came home and saw me there, he was in shock. He reminded me that he had told me to leave Philadelphia, but I told him if he didn't want me, he would have to learn to deal with it. I wasn't leaving until I could financially get myself together, because I had nowhere decent for Kesha and me to live. He left.

I think a big part of me was hoping he would change his mind and we could move past all the madness that I had suddenly found myself in. Once again, just as I had prayed about marrying him, I prayed and fasted again that God would change his mind, that he would once again love me like I thought he did. Reality is real and when you come to accept what is or what will be, you also have to learn how to deal with it. Now I was at a place in my little sanctified, Holy Ghost filled life that I had to accept and deal with the fact that George didn't love me like I loved him. He was living what came to be known as on the "down-low." He loved having sex with men. I think I could have competed if it had been other women, as we would have had the same tools to work with. But competing with another man? Naw!

# CHAPTER FIVE

By that time, I was totally embarrassed—and I do mean totally humiliated, uncomfortable, and self-conscious, because everyone at the church now knew that my marriage was destroyed. To make matters even worse was to find out that some of them knew about or suspected George's alternative lifestyle, which didn't include me or a child. Having a baby was his cover-up and having me as his wife made the cover-up easy to perform. Although I remained faithful in my church attendance and singing in the choir, I couldn't help but believe that people were laughing and talking about my failed marriage. Sometimes while attending services, all I had was my praise. During times of hurt, pain, and feeling like a failure, all I had was my praise and faith in God that He would somehow bring me through this turmoil.

When I say that I was filled with regret and yes, hatred toward George, it really is an understatement. I never degraded him to his daughter, though, and I was careful not to disrespect her by disrespecting him in front of her. Whenever Kesha would ask about him, my response would be to refer to him as "your father," but for more than twenty-one years I could only refer to him to others as "what's his face." Whenever I tried to say his name, I would literally begin to choke.

I preached, taught, and conducted revivals, youth seminars,

and single men's and women's seminars and conferences. I preached in Cheyenne, Wyoming; Los Angeles, California; and conducted revivals in Houston, Texas, and Washington, DC. I was used by God to lay hands on people, prophetically speak into their lives, and pray them into their deliverance. As I laid hands, people would come back with reports of being healed from cancer, ya da, ya da, ya da. Although I was bound up within myself, I kept praising God, praying, and fasting. God was opening doors for me in a way that was, and continues, to blow my mind. To God be the Glory! It was during this time of my brokenness that I began to understand Joel's prophecy: *"...I will pour out my Spirit upon all flesh; and your sons and your daughters shall prophesy, your old men shall dream dreams, your young men shall see visions: and also upon the servants and upon the handmaids in those days will I pour out my spirit."* (Joel 2:28-29)

As a child, I had seen God use male preachers in mighty ways. Growing up in the church, women (for a lack of a better term) were not acknowledged in ministry to the same degree as men. Coming to Philadelphia was an eye opener for me as far as seeing women take on leading roles in ministry and men recognizing that God can use whomever He chooses. It was also encouraging for me as a young licensed evangelist in the Church of God in Christ to sit with great female leaders such as the Late Mother Irene Oakley and Mother Elsie Shaw. Mother Oakley sat me down some years ago during one of the Commonwealth of Pennsylvania Convocations after I had preached at a youth service and gave me some pointers that have helped me in ministry. One thing that Mother Oakley said to me was, "Baby, I can help you, if you let me."

Those somewhat simple words have stuck with me like Crazy

# OUCH

Glue. I recall as a child hearing about the prayer mantle prophetic call of Mother Elsie Shaw. During my first year in attendance at the National Convocation in Memphis, Tennessee, I sat in awe at how Mother Shaw would pray and how God would prophetically speak through her. After my third time of attending the Convocation, I had purposed in my mind that I needed to get to Mother Shaw. I found what hotel she was staying in, and when I called that hotel I was connected to her room.

When Mother picked up the phone, she did not say hello. Instead she said, "You're from Philadelphia. The Lord told me to expect your call." She went right into prayer and began to speak of things I had and would have to endure "for the sake of the call of ministry on my life." She told me how the enemy would attack my health and how God would open doors for me that no man would be able to take credit for. Mother ended the call by telling me to make sure I got near her that night before she left Mason Temple, because God told her she had to lay hands on me and release the prayer mantle of my father on my life. I worship only God, but I honor the memory of these patriots and some that are still alive today.

# CHAPTER SIX

In 1974, I began to experience excruciating pain in my wrist while working at Methodist Hospital. At times I would be unable to move it, and the pain would be sharp and unbearable. There were times at church I would scream out because the pain was so great. I went to see Dr. Phil Marone, who at the time was the orthopedic specialist for the Philadelphia Phillies. He used steroid injections and put me in a cast for six weeks, and eventually told me he didn't think I was in as much pain as I was. In October of 1974, Dr. Marone operated on my wrist, and when I woke up from anesthesia he was sitting at the foot of my bed. He told me he wanted to be the first face I saw because he needed to apologize to me. When he opened my wrist, the tendons had wrapped around the bone in my wrist and a procedure that should have taken fifteen minutes took him two hours to correct.

By 1976, Kesha was still sleeping in a crib. One day, I picked her up and immediately dropped her back into the crib. My other wrist had the same symptoms. It did not matter where I was; when my hand would lock, I would scream out in pain–even in church. The pain was almost indescribable. So, once again, I found myself in the hospital having another surgery. I had not returned to work after having Kesha and when George left, I had no money and found myself on welfare. I felt degraded and

# OUCH

embarrassed, but I had to do what I had to do in order to take care of my daughter.

I enrolled into Philadelphia Community College in 1977 and lasted one semester. I took general studies because I really had no idea what I wanted to major in, but I was not mentally prepared for college at that time. My focus was more on getting a job so that I could financially take care of my responsibilities as a mother. In October of 1977, I was hired by Veterans Hospital of Philadelphia. I was so happy that things would be better, but by that time I was so behind in my rent it would take about three or four months of my entire bring-home pay to catch up. Kesha's godfather, Jim, and his wife offered me a place to stay in their home until I could save money and get another place of my own. I was so grateful and yet I felt that I was imposing on their family.

As I came home one night after working the 3pm to 11pm shift, Jim was sitting in his recliner waiting for me. We talked and agreed that it was time for me to look for a place of my own – no hard feelings, no bad blood. I began to diligently look for a place for my daughter and me. The next day at work, I told one of my co-workers, Cynthia, that I needed to find a place to live but I didn't want to live in Philly. I could not afford to send Kesha to private school, but I knew I wanted her to have a good education. During lunch, I bought a newspaper and checked the apartment section. I came across an ad for an apartment in what was then known as Cornwell Heights, Pennsylvania. When I made a phone call, they told me they just happened to have one two-bedroom available.

Cynthia and I took a ride to find this place called Cornwell Heights. There were no GPS or MapQuest directions available at that time; all I had was a determination to get there. I applied and within two weeks I was moving into my new apartment. My friend, Dill, was right there with me lifting boxes and helping me get settled.

Kesha went to Buffalo, New York, every summer to spend time with my family. One Sunday morning in August 1985, I got up to get ready for Sunday church services. That morning, I walked into the bedroom and crawled my way back out. In those days we went to Sunday School, morning service, and sometimes afternoon and evening services. My pastor at that time was the late Elder Paul F. Berry, known as a "preacher's preacher." He always told us if we were sick and needed to go to the hospital to call him so he could be praying for us. This Sunday, I called the church and was asked if I was on my way to church. I told the person I was sick and on my way to the emergency room. I was told that Elder Berry was getting ready to go into the sanctuary and he didn't have time to talk with me. I was in shock and severe pain at the same time.

When I got to the hospital, they ran tests and told me they had to operate immediately, or I would die. My appendix had burst. Terrified and all alone, I knew it was time for evening service so I figured I would try one more time to reach my pastor. One of the young people answered the phone this time, and I told her I needed to speak to Elder Berry. Her response was that he was in the pulpit. My response was, "Girl, go and tell Elder Berry I am in the hospital and it doesn't look good. I just want him to pray for me." When Elder Berry came to the phone, he asked me what was going on and where was I. Later, I found out that Pastor Berry went out into the church service and had the saints pray for me. The next morning after surgery, I opened my

# OUCH

eyes to see Elder Berry and Elder Hoffman standing at the foot of my bed. As happy as I was that they had come to check on me, the fact that I was unable to speak to him on my first call was hurtful. In case I didn't mention it earlier, let me say it now (and probably will say it again), there is no hurt like church hurt.

Because the illness was so unexpected, I had to wait six to eight weeks before my disability insurance coverage kicked in. Once again, I was falling behind in rent and other household bills. One of the deacons went to the head deacon to see if the church could help me, and he was told no. I later found out that I hadn't been at the church or paid enough tithes and offerings for the church to help me out. OUCH! One thing I had learned about God and why I love Him so very much is because of His word that declares: "Fear not, nor be afraid of them: for the Lord thy God, he it is, that go with thee; he will not fail thee, nor forsake thee." (Deuteronomy 31:6b) God will make a way and provide for His people.

He proved that when Evangelist Patricia Blount came to me and asked, "How much is your rent?" Completely blown away, I told her. She took out her checkbook and wrote a check payable to my landlord. When I got back on my feet and tried to repay her, she refused to take anything. She said, "I had to obey God, and He didn't tell me to loan you anything, He told me to pay your rent."

In 1985, I was informed about a better job opportunity. I applied and got hired at Children's Hospital of Philadelphia. I didn't have a car so when I worked the morning shift, I would have to leave my house at 4:45am. It was a twenty- minute walk to the nearest bus stop and I would arrive to work at 6:55am. Coming home was the same; I would get off at 3:00am and get home 5:45am. Needless to say, Kesha was a latch-key kid. For the most part of her life, it was just her and I. George hardly spent any time with her, but God would put godly men in my life that became my brothers and became uncles to her as well.

I worked a lot of overtime at CHOP, mainly because I wanted to give Kesha things in life that my parents were not able to give me or my sisters. I wanted her to have a good life, so I had to do what I had to do. I started going to Child Support Court at 1801 Vine Street in Philadelphia when Kesha was two years old, and did so faithfully until she was thirteen. Many of my visits to 1801 consisted of me being cursed out and even threatened by George. One time, they restrained me from leaving after the judge's ruling. The judge asked if George had any doubt that Kesha Marie Sellers was his daughter. Without hesitation, George acknowledged he had no doubt that Kesha was his daughter. He would come to court with a lawyer and dressed sharply in a three-piece suit. I came to court with God on my side.

The judge turned his attention to me and asked if I had anything to say before he made his ruling. I said, "Your Honor, Mr. Sellers is a preacher. If you lock him up until my daughter turns eighteen, I promise you, I will never come back to ask for one dime." George was outraged that his paycheck was going to be garnished. He suggested to the judge that since I was working and had a good job, he didn't feel he should have to pay child support. The judge picked up the file and spoke on the fact of how many times we had been to court. His ruling was for George to pay $132 every two weeks and that his check would be garnished since he refused to pay on his own.

When I say that George Sellers went completely off in that courtroom, I was called everything you can imagine and then

# OUCH

some. An officer suggested that, for my protection, I should stay for an hour to make sure he had gone. I cried, yes, cried real tears. Not because I was scared, and I had already reached my level of rejection and disrespect. So why was I crying? I'm glad you asked. I cried because I couldn't get to George. If I had, I honestly think that I would have tried to clean Vine Street with him, in his three-piece suit.

# CHAPTER SEVEN

By 1994, I had undergone two wrist surgeries. The top hand surgeon at the University of Pennsylvania told me that eventually I was going to lose complete use of my hands. In addition to the wrist surgery, I had carpal tunnel release in both hands, trigger thumb release, bone spur removal on both feet, and four surgeries on the toes of both feet. In 1999, I had an emergency hysterectomy; in 2000, I had my right knee replaced, and approximately six years later I had left knee replacement. By that time, I was receiving a little more than $700 a month in Social Security Disability–not enough to cover monthly expenses. Although I couldn't get a job in the secular world, my gift and calling as an evangelist helped sustain me.

In 1994, I felt God pulling me into a new direction. Although the Church of God in Christ was and remains my spiritual foundation, my heart and my desire to remain a member of Prayer and Faith Temple seemed to be decreasing. Yet, I didn't feel that God had given me a release to leave the ministry. The Late Bishop O.T. Jones served as Jurisdictional Presiding Prelate of the Commonwealth Jurisdiction of the COGIC, and Elder Ben Green was the State Youth President. I began working closely with Elder Green and the Youth Department.

At one of our state meetings on a Saturday afternoon, the

# OUCH

Youth Department held a service and Elder Green asked me to preach. The power of God was strong even before I got up to preach, which made preaching easy as I continued to flow in the already-present Spirit of God. While I was preaching, one of the senior elders walked up the center aisle and, with the motion of his hand, told me to stop preaching. I didn't want to be disobedient to the elder, but I felt such an anointing of the Holy Spirit. I looked at Elder Green. He said to me, "Follow God." Obeying the voice of God, I asked that seven people that were sick to come forth because I needed to lay hands on them.

The next year while attending another state function, a lady came to me from Harrisburg, Pennsylvania. She asked if I remembered her, to which I responded no. She went on to tell me how grateful she was that I had obeyed God the year before. She was scheduled to have a radical breast mastectomy that following Tuesday. She checked into the hospital on Monday and the doctor decided to run some more tests before taking her into the operating room on Tuesday. Her praise report was that the doctor's test revealed the cancer was now gone. All I could say was, "To God be the Glory!"

Around two years later, Elder Green and his wife started the All People Family Worship Center. I talked with Pastor Berry and told him I felt my time at PFT had come to an end. He said that he didn't want me to go, but if I felt this was what God was doing, he gave me his blessings. After having that conversation with Elder Berry, I became the first member to join this non-denominational church. God used Pastor Green to awaken and speak life into some spiritual gifts that I did not realize I had, or ones I was afraid to allow God to use in or through me. After all, back then women were not used or recognized in ministry as they are today. While at All Peoples Family Worship Center, I was faithful and worked hard to serve my leaders, just as I had done in the past. However, as I often say, "There is no perfect church because we are an imperfect people." Again, I say church hurt is like no other hurt.

At APFWC, I was placed over the Intercessory Prayer Ministry by Pastor Green, who was indeed a man of prayer. My responsibility was not just to get people to pray but to understand what being an intercessor meant. We became known as All People Intercessory Prayer Ministry. Once again, I felt God was revealing Himself to me in a way I never thought I would be used. I came up with the idea of sowing financially into the lives of our pastor and first lady on the third Sunday of each month. I became part of the leadership that took on the responsibility of sending Pastor and First Lady to the Bahamas for a week.

Slowly but surely, things began to change at APFWC. One day, I had been given instructions to pass on to one of the young people. I did and said exactly what I was told to do, however, I did not realize that there would be problem. But there was a problem, and those involved complained. I was called into a meeting with Pastor and First Lady, where I gladly repeated what I had been asked to do and the response I got, which appeared to be favorable. The young people, however, had complained, and I was rebuked and humiliated before other leaders and made to look bad for doing something good.

On a Tuesday evening in December of 1998, I met with Pastor to talk about the direction I thought God was now taking me. Granted, I never wanted or desired to be a pastor. That night when I met with Pastor, I shared what I believed to be God's new direction for my life. He rejoiced and told me he was

# OUCH

going to meet with me about starting a work in Bensalem, Pennsylvania. I just wanted to start with having a weekly Bible study and see where it would lead.

Because I had preached in several areas in New Jersey as well as in Brooklyn and the Bronx in New York, a friend wanted to put on a service to help financially start this ministry. I told Pastor Green about the service and he seemed to agree with it. As a matter of fact, he told me that my Philadelphia church family was going to come to the Bronx for support. At some point a letter was sent out about this service. It was a letter I have never, ever seen, but I was told it said something like: "Join us in the planting of the Lord's work." The Saturday before the third Sunday in March of 1999, I received a call from my pastor. Long story short, he told me that on Sunday he was going to release me from the ministry. I was heartbroken to say the least, devastated at its worst, but since then I never backed down from a fight or bullies.

I went to church that Sunday, and to my surprise I was called up to stand before the entire congregation when it happened: Pastor Green announced that I was no longer a leader and they were not to listen to anything I had to say. I thought he would take me into his office after service to tell me this, but it seemed to me that he, for whatever reason, wanted to humiliate me, and that he did. After service on that Sunday, people that would usually greet me with a hug walked by me like I had a deadly disease. Not only had I lost my pastor, but the distance between my brother and I was immeasurable.

I would see people that once told me how much they loved me now not even speak to me. It wasn't the first time I had been ridiculed for trying to do something good in church. My previous church at times had made me feel so unworthy, displaced, and at times unloved except for the young people and one or two of the church mothers. I never dreamt that I would experience it again, especially from someone I considered to be my brother before he became my pastor.

With all the physical surgeries I had, the healing pain was more intense and took longer with some more than the others. I have been in an operating room more than forty-three times, and even with some form of anesthesia, dealing with the apprehension of going into the operating room and not knowing how or if I would come out the way I went in was quite overwhelming, to say the least. However, the pain that comes from church hurt is far more painful, more stressful, and the recovery time cannot be estimated. Church hurt just really hurts, and many times the pain of it goes to the very core of your heart.

# CHAPTER EIGHT

On Wednesday, April 14, 1999, I held a gathering at the Holiday Inn Hotel in Bensalem, Pennsylvania. The purpose of this meeting was to present a vision for the Bensalem Worship Center. There were about thirty people in attendance, and I explained to them that my desire was to simply teach the Word of God in a relaxed, non-traditional way, with the intent to get people to accept Jesus as their Lord and Savior and build a personal relationship with Him.

For about three months things went well. Bible study was well attended, people were learning God's Word, and some were applying it to their lives. There were times that, whatever I had scheduled to teach, evidently God had other plans. On some occasions, the worship would be so intense that some would kneel, some would lay prostrate before God, others would sit and weep, and others would get up and walk. Bensalem Worship Center was established on prayer, the Word, and worship.

When we decided to move forward from just having Bible study to holding Sunday worship services, the attendance increased, and membership started to grow. The services were encouraging, and the presence and power of God was phenomenal. God manifested Himself through healings and prophetically speaking to his people. There were some people that joined the church that had never been in a church. One young lady came to BWC because she was a friend of my daughter's and had been invited. When she finally came, I did not realize that she did not believe that God existed. I recall doing a four-week study on the "Names of God." By the end of that teaching I asked the question, "What name of God is He in your life?" Her response was, "To me He is Jehovah-Shalom. He has given me peace and tranquility that I never experienced until I started coming here." Needless to say, just about everyone was in tears that night.

As time continued to move forward, our Bible study attendance began to drop tremendously. Sunday services were still being well attended, but eventually that dropped as well. I remember preaching one Sunday morning and Kesha was the only one in attendance that day. While I was preaching, she got up to go to the restroom and I kept preaching to the chairs. When she returned, it was as if we never missed a beat.

While I continued trying to grow the ministry, I had my first total knee replacement, which caused me to be out of commission for about six weeks. Thankfully, the presiding prelate of the organization I was a part of sent one of the elders from his church to preach in my stead. Eventually, the membership, which had grown to approximately one hundred and twenty-five, decreased to about four. I had to come to grips with the fact that I needed to close the Bensalem Worship Center. I was heartbroken and blamed myself. I tried to figure out what I had done wrong or if there was something I should or should not have done. Depression set in deep!

There were so many questions I asked God: "Was I wrong for trying to pastor a church? Am I outside of Your will for my life?" I felt like such a failure. I didn't join another church but

## OUCH

kept busy running revivals and teaching at different conferences. Inside, I was broken. Once again, I felt like I was the laughing-stock of the church people. I had pastors ask me to join their church to help them out, but I didn't want to be a member of anyone's church, so my answer was always "No." Thinking back on it, I was leery and very apprehensive of being hurt once again by church folk, and yet it happened–again.

I finally started attending a church near Philadelphia on a regular basis. I sat with the pastor and explained that I had no intention of joining his church, that I simply came because I enjoyed their service. Although he said he understood and would be glad to have me attend the services, there were Sundays when I would come and he would put me up to preach the sermon. Being raised in the church, that was not that surprising, as my father would do it from time to time if visiting another church. This, however, was different. I would purposely get to the service late and it was apparent that the praise team would wait until I walked in and I would be announced as the morning preacher. Tuesday night Bible studies became the same cycle, where I would show up after driving forty-five miles from work only to find out when I got there that I was being asked to preach.

It got to a point that I was before the people more than their pastor, which caused them to start coming to me for answers to issues that should have been taken to their pastor. I've never been one to like or deal with drama, so I began to distance myself from that church. A few of those members expressed their desire to follow me wherever I went, and once again I considered starting a Bible study in my home. I discouraged them from leaving their home church because, once again, I wasn't sure what outcome to expect and I didn't want to be considered as "stealing someone's members."

Somehow, the pastor got word that I was planning to start a Bible study and was encouraging his members to leave his church to become a part of what I was doing. Mind you, I was only thinking of starting a Bible study and never joined that church. But once again, I faced humiliation when I was told that this pastor put the word out that I was starting a "gay church."

OUCH, that one hurt real bad. I could not understand how people who said they loved God had no problem with scandalizing another person's character and reputation. Although my marriage had failed, I was divorced, and had not been on a date with another man, being gay was not a desire of mine nor the will of God. It is amazing how people in the church will label you based on their perception. If you are a female and they see you with females, you get classified as a lesbian. If you are a man and are always seen with men, they you are considered gay or a homosexual. Not that there are many cases that that is true, but for me that definitely was not the case. I realized it was best that I disconnected myself from that ministry as well as that pastor.

Once again, there I was, not regularly attending any church, and I was good with that. At the time I was overweight, almost three hundred pounds and five feet four inches tall. I would often say, and continue to say, "I may not preach that good, but I preach hard." I didn't realize what was going on in my physical body during this journey. I had been hospitalized three times, for three or four days at a time, with all the systems of having a heart attack. But thanks be unto God, I was never diagnosed with a heart attack. My doctors told me I needed to slow down

## OUCH

and rest. What? How could I rest when I had revivals to conduct, conferences to attend, Women's Day services to preach? Rest was not on my calendar.

# CHAPTER NINE

My "queen," my mother, had to have her right leg her amputated, but that never stopped her. She continued to travel to the national COGIC conventions, especially the women's convention. She also endured several strokes but fought hard to bounce back, and that she did. My baby sister, Cat, began to get sick with diabetes, but too she was a trooper. As time went on, she became sicker and sicker, doctor visit after doctor, hospitalized time and time again. Finally, after suffering for fifteen years, she got a diagnosis of multiple sclerosis (MS). By the time she received the diagnosis, she had practically lost the use of her legs and needed to be in a wheelchair. On February 8, 2002, I received a call that Cat had passed away. She was the first member of my immediate family to pass away and our family, including her three children, were devastated.

Almost immediately after Cat's death, my father's health also began to decline, and my mother had another stroke. Reverend's (what we called my father) diabetes was out of control. He lost his eyesight and hearing but continued to try to carry on the church. Dementia also set in, but my mom refused to put him in a nursing home. It seemed like when Cat died, a major part of him died with her and he was never the same. On November 4, 2004, while I was on the phone talking with my

# OUCH

mom, she told me that she had just gotten home from visiting with Reverend at the hospital and she didn't think he would be around much longer. Sure enough, as we were still talking, Buffalo General Hospital called her. She put me on hold and when she returned, she told me that Reverend had just passed away.

That was late on a Saturday night, but first thing Sunday morning I was in my car and on my way to Buffalo. The month of November is known as National/International Convocation in Memphis, Tennessee, and because so many people that respected my father had already left for Memphis while others were leaving that Monday, my mom's desire was to wait until they returned to have his homegoing service. Whatever Mom wanted was what we were going to do. My father left a legacy of prayer, which many of us still walk in this day.

I believe I stated before, and I will continue to say as long as long as I live, that my mother was the strongest black woman I will ever know. Her health was failing, but she remained faithful to the church. I had to literally move her out of the church parish because it was too much for her to handle. By that time, she was suffering with rheumatoid arthritis in her crippled hands; except for one finger, her hand stayed curled in a ball shape. One day my cousin, Lena, went to check on her only to find her on the floor after having yet another stroke. The doctors said she would not bounce back from this one, but they really did not know Martha.

She went into rehab in Buffalo and it broke my heart because she felt that Mary and I were throwing her away. I quickly began to investigate rehab facilities in Bensalem, Pennsylvania, and I found one about seven minutes from my house. The arrangements were made, and along with Lena and her son, Lil Joe, we drove her to Pennsylvania. I was working for the Trenton Board of Education and every day after work, I went by to check on Mom. I would even get up at 2am or 3am just to check on my mother to make sure she was being properly taken care of.

One morning, one of the workers refused to answer the call bell when Mom had an accident. She cried all day. When I got there after work, one of the aides told me what happened (overall the staff was very good to Mom). She went on to tell me that she advised that particular aide not to come to work that night, stating, "Grandma's daughter is going to come up here looking for you tonight and you don't need to be there." She was right. I got up at 1:30am and went to confront the woman, and sure enough, she called out that night. Thank God, because I probably would have gotten charged.

The next day, I requested a meeting with every director of that facility, where I expressed my displeasure of how my mother was treated. I went on to tell them that the individual who refused to give my mom a bedpan, and when she got around to it raised her voice at my mother, no longer needed to work there and perhaps they should relieve her of her duties. It was just a suggestion, but evidently they agreed, and she was relieved of her duties at that facility.

## CHAPTER TEN

Taking on the responsibility of a full-time health care-giver, while working a full time job and fulfilling ministerial engagements, can be overwhelming or, should I say, very overwhelming. Although my daughter was very helpful and a nurse came in for a few hours a day, the weight of that responsibility was still a lot. But when it came to my mom, I did what I had to do and would do it again, if she were still here with us. Like many of the older saints that I grew up under, they seemed to look forward to "going home to be with the Lord." Sometimes they would say, "I'm living to live again," and Mom's favorite was: "When my train pulls in and the conductor says 'ALL ABOARD,' I'm going tell him, 'I got my ticket and I'm ready to go.'" I used to hate hearing her say that. After all, we know that, unless the rapture comes first, we all will leave this earth one day. Thank God the train was delayed for several years.

Mom, being as determined as she was, moved back to Buffalo, New York, because she wanted to be around her friends and the saints she was familiar with. My nephew, Lawrence, came to Bensalem at Mom's request and took her back to Buffalo, where he became her caretaker. Being a very determined and independent woman, she did what could to take care of herself. The rheumatoid arthritis in her hands became more and more crippling, at times making it difficult for her to place a slice of bread in the toaster without crumbling the bread into pieces. Her diabetes, which caused her to lose her right leg, was affecting her left foot, leaving her without a heel. It was heart-wrenching to see Mom endure such pain, unable to wear any kind of shoe, and yet her faith in God remained unshaken. She would always encourage Mary, me, and others, young and old, to "pray."

Over the years I made several trips to Buffalo, checking on Mom and spending time with other family members. With Mom not being able to walk and confined to a wheel chair, it became difficult for her to be transported back and forth to church. Although she could not make it to church, she remained faithful with her tithe and offerings and other required obligations. There would be times when her body would be wracked with pain, but I never recalled her complaining. Her favorite two songs that she would sing in her strong alto voice were, "I know the Lord, will make a way, Oh, yes He will," and "Just another day that the Lord has kept me, just another day that the Lord has kept me. He has kept me from all evil with my mind stayed on Jesus, it's just another day that the Lord has kept me." Mom taught me how to love God in the midst of heartache, disappointment, and unpleasant circumstances and situations. When I felt broken, I could call on Mom. Sometimes she came with correction, sometimes rebuke, but no matter what, the conversation would always end with, "I love you and don't stop praying."

# CHAPTER ELEVEN

On November 25, 2008, while working for the Trenton Board of Education as a security officer at one of the high schools, I was on my lunch break when a fight broke out at the bottom of the stairs that I just happened to be walking down. Two other security officers had broken up the fight between the two boys, but one of the boys was aggressively trying to get back to finish the fight. John, the security officer, had a strong hold on the kid but he was determined to resume the fight. As I was standing against the wall that led to one of the school's entrances, I could tell they were going to fall. I screamed out, "John, be careful you're going to fall!" And fall they did, about four hundred pounds right into my shoulder, tearing my right rotator cuff.

In January of 2009, I had my first rotator cuff repair surgery. Approximately two weeks later I was in physical therapy. Just to let you know, therapy on a shoulder is very intense, and very, and I do mean very, painful. After the first two weeks of therapy, I was back into surgery for what is called "frozen shoulder." Therapy started all over for following nine months, three days a week. Many of those days I was in tears but determined to regain normal use of my right arm.

In 2012, I was back in surgery on the same shoulder after being told that the rotator cuff had disconnected and had to be repaired once again, which also meant going back into therapy for another nine months. Again in 2015, I began having difficulty raising my right arm; even sleeping on my right side was difficult. That time, I was sent to another doctor who told me that my shoulder was so messed up that the only thing left to do was a total shoulder replacement. I didn't even know they did such a thing. It was the fourth time I was in surgery for my right shoulder, always followed by months of intense painful therapy.

On February 29, 2016, we celebrated my son-in-law's birthday. His actual birthday was on the 27th, but with schedules being the way they were, we celebrated on that Tuesday night. I made ham, Cornish hens, collard greens, macaroni and cheese, and homemade stuffing. Mike loved when I cooked like that.

Kesha got home from work, and we sat around the dining room table laughing and just having a fun time, which we often did. Michael treated me like a mother and I him as if he was my natural son. On March 1, he left early in the morning while Kesha was in the process of getting dressed for work. I had just gotten home from my overnight shift and went straight to bed when Kesha came into my room. "Mom, Mike was in an accident! I'm going to the hospital to see him." I replied, "Ok, let me know if I need to come down."

Kesha called approximately ten minutes after leaving the house. I could tell she was crying. "Mom, they said he's not breathing." Immediately I jumped up, got in the shower, got dressed, and within five minutes was out the door. Figuring it was going to be a long day at the hospital, I stopped by Dunkin Donuts to grab a cup of coffee. As I was pulling away from the drive-thru window my phone rang again, this time with Kesha screaming as she told me that Mike was dead!

# OUCH

I literally almost lost control of my car. I could not believe, or should I say, I did not want to believe, what I had heard. When I arrived at the hospital, I told the guard who I was there to see but he would not let me go into the room. I was getting as hot as fish grease. Finally, someone came out to escort me into the triage room. When he opened the door and saw my son lying on the stretcher, not breathing, it was unbearable. Mike had gotten hit in the back of his head with a ton of trash.

My daughter was a mess and so was I. Clearly, I know what has been taught about grief and how we, as believers, are expected to act, but let me tell you this: all of that went right out the door. I made several phone calls, and the people that I hold dear to my heart were right there for me. My sister/ friend, Bishop Pamela Herndon, drove up from North Carolina the same day, stayed overnight, went back to Raleigh and returned for the funeral services. Apostle Pat Phillips did not hesitate, as well as many others. I thank God for the people that He has put in my life, people that are genuine and understand the true meaning of friendship.

# CHAPTER TWELVE

By 2017, I not only had metal in both knees but also metal in my right shoulder, which came with a list of weight restrictions pertaining to how much I could push, pull or lift. Indeed, I was in a state of depression once again. I even questioned God as to how much more I had to go through? A question He has yet to answer; after all, He is still God and sovereign. After having my secret pity party, I made up my mind that I am a SURVIVOR! I was determined to get through this, hence my email address, "I was made-two-survive and survive I will do." By 2019, all I could pray was, Not again, God, please not another surgery. No, not just one but three.

I went through a period of being extremely tired and out of breath. I would be standing up preaching and it would seem like my breath was actually leaving my body. There were times when my daughter would recognize what was happening and would come in the pulpit and place a chair behind me to keep me from falling. Several times at home I would walk out of my bedroom and find myself having passed out on the floor. To be honest, with all the Jesus I have, it was scary.

Finally, my heart doctor recommended I have a nuclear stress test. I scheduled the test, which could take two to three hours to complete. When I arrived at the testing site, they explained the

# OUCH

procedure to me part by part. After they put the IV in my arm they called for me to come back in for part two thirty minutes later. Thanks be unto God, instead of them injecting me with the dye, they hooked me up to the EKG machine. Suddenly, the technician hollered, "STOP!" I lay there, thinking a lead had become disconnected. The supervisor was notified, and she came and told the technician to start up the machine again. Soon after she yelled, "Stop, unplug her now! Do it now!" Somewhat nervous, I sat up and asked what was wrong; I was told I needed to see an electrophysiologist. What is that, you wonder? That's the same thing I asked them, but I was told to go home and they would call me. By the time I got home the cardiac care unit called me, telling me I had an appointment the next day and I needed to keep it. By that time, my nerves were on edge. I had sleepless night, loss of appetite, and much more.

The next day when I went to my appointment, the doctor came out, introduced himself, and hooked me up again to the EKG machine. This time the doctor yelled, "STOP! Disconnect her now!" "Okay, what the heck is going on?" is my question. The doctor began to ask me a list of questions: "How did you get here? How did you get into the building? Who came with you?" My answers were that I drove myself, I walked from the parking lot into the building, walked to the elevator, pushed the button for the third floor, got off the elevator, and made a left turn into the office. The look of amazement on his face was amazing. He told me I should not have been able to do any of those things because my body was in "flat line mode," meaning that my heart rate was in the low twenties. I needed a pacemaker and I needed it as soon as possible. On June 3, 2019, I was in surgery having a pacemaker put in my chest. Thank God for life.

Still in 2019, my right knee replacement is twenty years old. The orthopedic doctor performed x-rays which showed that all the metal that was put in twenty years ago needed to be replaced in what is called a revised total knee replacement, which is more detailed than the original. In August, once again I was in surgery and back in therapy. Surely this is it, I thought, not another surgery. Wrong. My right shoulder once again was causing me excruciating pain. What could possibly be wrong now?

You ever feel like enough is enough? Well, I'm here to tell you that enough is not always enough. God's plan for our lives far exceeds what we can imagine. I made an appointment to see my shoulder doctor, who ordered an MRI and CT scan, only to tell me that there was no more rotator cuff to repair. She needed to go back into my right shoulder and put a metal rotator cuff in or else I will lose total use of my right arm. By November of 2019, surgery number forty-three.

# CHAPTER THIRTEEN

By that time, I had received a phone call from Texas. I was that my sister, Mary, had been diagnosed with fourth stage advanced pancreatic cancer that had metastasized to other organs in her body. My first words were, "Oh my God, you have got to be kidding me. This cannot be happening."

I had to go to rehab for my shoulder because if I didn't the surgeon would have to go back in to correct what is known as frozen shoulder release. And since the doctor had already told me that there was nothing else that she could do for my arm and that I would lose total use of it, it was made very plain that from that point on for the rest of my life I would be limited in what I could pull, push, or lift. To be exact, she said no more than seven pounds and that was a stretch. As of now, if I hold a baby, the baby has to be placed in my left arm. I knew I had to get some therapy under my belt. I knew I was going to have to push and push myself in my therapy sessions, both at home and at the rehab site. There were times when my therapist would tell me to slow down, I was doing too much to soon. I was farther along than I should be after having had this kind of shoulder surgery, which in case I didn't mention before is a major surgery.

I would pray and take pain pills to help me get through these sessions. Sometimes tears would run down my face, but I had a determination to keep pushing forward. There are times in life, when faced with difficult challenges, that you have to tell yourself that, no matter how hard, how painful, or how discouraging things may get, "I am determined to push my way through this. I may have to cry through the process but with God's help and His strength, I am determined to come out of this on the other side."

While I was going through therapy, my sister/cousin, Vet, flew down to Texas to look after Mary. My daughter Kesha took two weeks of leave from her job and also flew down to Texas, which allowed me time to consecrate my shoulder and the healing process associated with it. By January I had stopped therapy, which neither my doctor nor therapist were in agreement with, but I felt I needed to go to Houston so that I could see for myself how Mary was really doing. I stayed in Texas from January until mid-March. I didn't mind, but because of how my mother raised us, I did what I had and needed to do.

I was back home by the middle of March, and once again Vet took off from her job and went back to Texas. By April 3, I too was back on a plane to Texas after receiving a call that Mary had developed a blood clot. My God, what else can happen? Yes, and for those of you who think that God should not be questioned I make no apologies, because my relationship with my Heavenly Father gives me the right to ask why, how long, how come, when is this going to end? and the list goes on and on. But please understand, although I ask Him does not mean that He always answers.

I honestly feel that God has a sense of humor and that He wants to see us laugh at times. The Bible says, *"a cheerful heart is good medicine, but a broken spirit saps a person's strength." (Proverbs 17:22; Life Application Study Bible)*. I promise you, a good laugh every now

## OUCH

and then will do you good. As of right now, I can say Mary is doing well and has already outlived the six to nine-month life span that the oncologist gave her. To God be the glory!!

# CHAPTER FOURTEEN

In 2018, I visited Liberated Word Ministry in Trenton, New Jersey, where my friend and brother, Pastor Michael Coe, serves as the pastor. On this particular Sunday he had quest preachers (husband and wife) minister. The wife spoke from St. Matthew 18:21-22, which says: "Then came Peter to him, and said, Lord how oft shall my brother sin against me, and I forgive him? Till seven times? Jesus saith unto him, I say not unto thee, until seven times; but until seventy times seven."

As she continued to expound on the Word, she began to talk about how the power of unforgiveness for the individual that refuses to forgive can become a toxic weight and even a form of bondage for that individual. As she continued to preach, she expressed how forgiveness is more for the person that has been hurt or done wrong than it is for the one that has caused the pain. By that time, I was crying like a child who just got the worst spanking of their life. I literally turned my face to the wall and asked God to forgive me for being unforgiving. Once I prayed that prayer, it seemed like God began to download in my memory the church people that had lied on me, put labels on me, or said mean and evil words to me. People I had tried to be there for when they needed me, but when the table was turned, they were either nowhere to be found or too busy to be bothered.

# OUCH

After church, tears were still running down my face as I sat in my car to go home. I recalled asking God how was it that He would use and anoint me to speak words of encouragement to others, all while knowing that I was in the same state of mind that they were. For so long preachers give the impression that their lives are perfect and they don't make mistakes or have to ask God for forgiveness. Please don't be offended, but I am not that preacher. I realize that you can't tell everything, but in these over fifty six years that I have been preaching, I have found that one of the best ways to get a message across is by not just preaching at the people but including yourself in the message. After all, my father would tell us, the Word comes to you first and then you give it to the people.

That following Monday, I started making calls to people that had acted shady towards me and asked them that, if I had done or said anything to them, to please forgive me. Some replied that I never did anything to them, while others replied, "It's about time you came to me. Now I can come hear you preach," while others seemed to have no idea what I was talking about. The amazing thing about my forgiveness is that whatever their response was, it didn't matter. I was walking in freedom and unforgiveness, and I was completely and totally free.

Not! "Come on God, you can't possibly want me to call George." I told myself I would forgive him in my heart and after twenty years I would no longer call him "what's his face." I could actually hear God's voice say to me, "It's all or nothing." Now I was angry with God. Yes, that's right, I repeat, I was angry with God! I figured, why do I have to say anything to him? I had already dealt with a period of low self-esteem because of this man who had belittled me in every way possible, and financially he hadn't taken care of me or our child. All those times I had to go to child support court to get him to give me a lousy $132 every two weeks, and he wasn't even consistent in doing that. God, I thought, why do I have to say anything to him?

God said nothing for the next two weeks. I would pray, read the Bible, and try to prepare a message to deliver to God's people, and still He said nothing. God had put me on shutdown. I thought I had passed the test when I went to other people, but how wrong I was – that was the ultimate test. I tried to convince myself that, as so many times before, George would hang up on me and that would get me off the hook. To be honest I still put it off. I believed I was afraid of opening myself to being hurt again, and if that happened, I didn't know how I would handle it. And prayer was not on the list of things to do.

Finally, I made the call. There was no answer, so I left a message and got no response. Okay, now I am really off the hook, God, I made an effort. After about two days I told Kesha I had tried to call and text her father. Yes, she was shocked. "Mom, you called my father, you all right?" A part of me knew she would get in touch with him to find out why he didn't respond. Well, as it turned out I had the wrong number, off by one digit. Oh my God, when is this going to be over? Kesha gave me the correct number, and once again I had no excuse.

I made the call, but did I mention I had once again built up a wall that would prevent him from ever hurting me again? My guns were ready to shoot back at anything negative that might have come out of his mouth. But to my surprise, he sounded humble and said he was glad to hear from me. "Well, Kesha told me that you had not been feeling well, so I just wanted to check

# OUCH

on you," I said. He thanked me for calling and that was the end of that, or so I thought.

In March of 2020, Kesha told me she wanted her grandfather and her dad to come for dinner and would I be okay with her father being there? I told her, "This is as much your house as it is mine, I will just stay in my room." I didn't find out until later that the other part of this gathering is that they wanted me to cook. Their menu consisted of baby lima beans, rice, fried chicken, and homemade pound cake.

On March 12, 2020, by the time Kesha's grandfather and father arrived the only thing left to cook for dinner was to fry the chicken. When I came downstairs, her grandfather, Buster, who turned ninety-two years old on his last birthday, jumped out of the recliner, ran towards me, and gave me the biggest hug. George, who could barely turn around and definitely could not jump out of anything, said hi, his voice just above a whisper, I replied, "How are you?" I could not believe how much he had aged or how sick he was. Not ready for this, my heart was touched at the physical condition he was in.

We had dinner, and after cleaning the kitchen I fixed to-go plates for them. After Kesha helped George put on his jacket he walked towards me, and before I knew it he had his arms around me, crying like a little boy whose train set just got broken. "I'm so sorry, I am so sorry, please forgive me," he said. I was totally caught off guard but I replied, "You're all right, you really need to take care of yourself." Kesha took George home while I sat with Buster, chatting and watching television. The evening ended much better than I had convinced myself it would.

# CHAPTER FIFTEEN

Once again just for clarity, I was totally caught off guard by George's reaction and his words. When Kesha returned home I went to my room, leaving her to entertain her grandfather. Once in my room, I sat on the side of the bed because by now I had to realize I was in a state of shock. I never thought I would hear those words come out of George's mouth. It had been over forty years since I had heard a kind word come across his lips to me. There had been times when we would run into each other at a funeral of someone from my past church, but there was no conversation.

Since God had dealt with me about forgiveness, I really felt that I was in a peaceful and safe place. I had let go of deep-seated anger that had really tormented me for years. I had long since overcome that journey of low self-esteem that I had embarked on forty-plus years ago, or so I tried to tell myself.

Of course, the devil was in my ear like a buzzing bumblebee; after all, he comes to destroy, kill, and steal. So in that moment, the devil brought up all the negativity, all the evilness, the breakdown of my self-esteem – which at one time was beyond low – and all the years of me questioning God about the path my life had taken. He brought up all the church people that had given me the impression that whatever I was going through was not

## OUCH

important and I just needed to get over it; the struggles I had endured so that my daughter would have a better life than I had; the people that I felt were necessary to have in my life because I wanted to feel like I belonged to someone. And then the devil began to remind me of all, and I do mean all, of the defaming words that George had spurred out of his mouth towards me, the rejection not only from George but from "church people." Those times when I would look at myself in the mirror and felt like I looked like a failure, was ugly and too fat, weighing almost 300 pounds at one time in my life, that one time when George almost became physical towards me, and the list went go on and on.

As I sat there on the side of my bed, I literally had to shut the devil and his words down. I began to pull down and saturate my mind with the words of God that had helped my through these things in the past, scriptures such as: "I will praise thee; for I am fearfully and wonderfully made: marvelous are thy works; and that my soul knoweth right well" (Psalm 139:14); "Hear my cry, O God; attend unto my prayer. From the end of the earth will I cry unto thee, when my heart is overwhelmed: lead me to the rock that is higher than I. For thou hast been a shelter for me and a strong tower from the enemy" (Psalms 61:1-3).

Again, God began to deal with me, knowing quite well that I was on my way back to that place of unforgiveness, a place I honestly never wanted to revisit. That place of bondage, low self-esteem, and anger. As I sat on my bed I knew I had to shut the devil down. I had learned to guard my ear-gate, so I decided to put what I had learned into practice. I began to pray that God would cover my mind and take control of my thoughts, and the presence of God filled my bedroom. Afterwards, I got my Bible and began to saturate my mind, my ears, and my tongue with scriptures that had helped me over the past forty plus years.

Seeing George had brought back such awful memories, but I had to continue walking in this season of what God was doing in my life. I could not or would not allow George or any evil force take me back to that place. I was and am determined to walk in the confidence that God has allowed me to embark upon. Sometimes when you have lived in a state of bondage, low self-esteem, and heartbreak, the enemy will do everything in his power to draw you back to that place.

I refused to allow Satan or any person to take me back to that place of "OUCH." I am confident in who I am and whose I am. I no longer allow people to weigh me down with their thoughts or opinion of me. I am not suggesting that the memory of the pain does not exist, but what I am declaring is that "IT DON'T HURT ANYMORE."

# EPILOGUE

I would just like to encourage anyone that has experienced hurt, disappointment, or faced some situation or circumstances that you didn't sign up for, to stay focused on God. Of course, it is sometimes better said than done, but I promise you firsthand, if he did it for me He can do it for you. It is most important and extremely necessary to maintain your trust in God, maintain your faith without wavering, and exercise the power of FORGIVENESS.

Again, I did not write OUCH to bash or defame anyone. I wrote it to tell my story, in hopes that someone that has been through some area of hurt can now understand that you can lift up your head because you survived.

*"Now thanks be unto God, which always causeth us to triumph in Christ,......" (2nd Corinthians 2:14)*

**Blessings**

www.ingramcontent.com/pod-product-compliance
Lightning Source LLC
LaVergne TN
LVHW021622080426
835510LV00019B/2711